CANNIBAL ANIMALS

JOHN PERRITANO

red rhino
bOOks®
NONFICTION

SADDLEBACK
EDUCATIONAL PUBLISHING
www.sdlback.com

ISBN-13: 978-1-68021-048-4
ISBN-10: 1-68021-048-3
eBook: 978-1-63078-367-9

Printed in Singapore by Craft Print International Ltd
0000/CA00000000

19 18 17 16 15   1 2 3 4 5

TABLE OF CONTENTS

2

Chapter 1

MAN-KILLER

There.

Sitting on a branch.

It looks like a stick.

A green one.

But it's not.

It's a praying mantis.

A male.

He's eating.

Then a female shows up.

The male looks.

He walks toward her.

Flaps his wings.

The female turns her head.
She jumps on him.
And pins him down.
He can't move.
The two mate.

She's not done.
She kills the male.
But death comes slowly.
The female bites his jaw.
Rips it. Chews it.
Next come his eyes.
She pulls them out.
Swallows them.
The male sits.
He won't fight back.

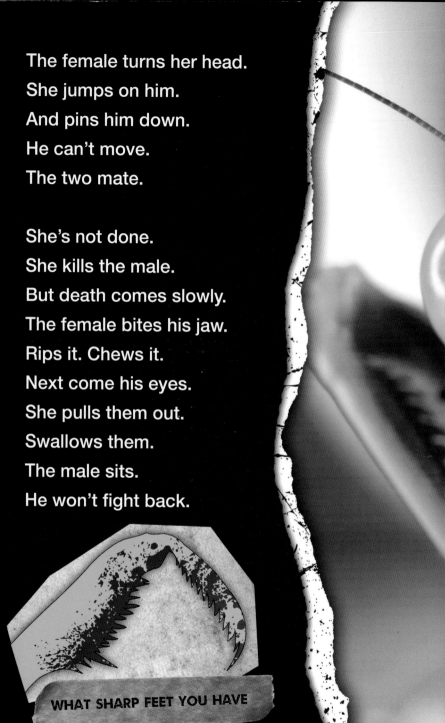

WHAT SHARP FEET YOU HAVE

5

The female is a *cannibal*.
She eats her own kind.

She's not alone.
Many animals do this.
Females eat males.
Parents eat children.
Sisters eat brothers.

To humans it's gross.
But not in the wild.
The weak come for dinner.
But never leave.

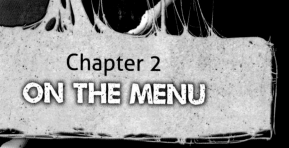

Chapter 2
ON THE MENU

Eating their own kind.

Some 1,500 animals do this.

It's part of nature.

Cannibals come in all sizes.

They can be cute.

Like dogs.

Chickens.

Chimps.

They can be cuddly.

Like hamsters.

Guinea pigs.

They can be scary.

Like alligators.

Sharks.

CUTE CANNIBALS

Household Cats

Mother cats eat sick kittens. They want healthy ones to survive.

Most live in water.

Oceans.

Rivers.

Lakes.

Many more are bugs.

Wasps.

Bees.

Beetles.

Some eat to live.

Or because Earth is warming.

Others eat just to eat.

Chapter 3
NUMBERS GAME

Orange Lake, Florida.

Alligator country.

Gators eat meat.

Snails.

Fish.

Birds.

Rats.

But food can run short.

What do some adults do?

They eat the young.

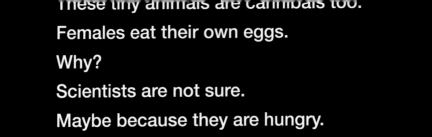

These tiny animals are cannibals too.
Females eat their own eggs.
Why?
Scientists are not sure.
Maybe because they are hungry.
And there is not much food.

CUTE CANNIBALS

Rabbits

So cute. So tidy. Mother bunnies eat their stillborn babies. It keeps their nests clean.

Chapter 4
EATING HEALTHY

Life in the wild is tough.
Animals have to be strong.
Healthy.
That's how they stay alive.
Eating their own can help them.
Make them stronger.

Bonobos.
African apes.
Scientists studied them.
They saw a female.
Olga.
She had two daughters.
Ophelia and Olivia.
Olivia died.

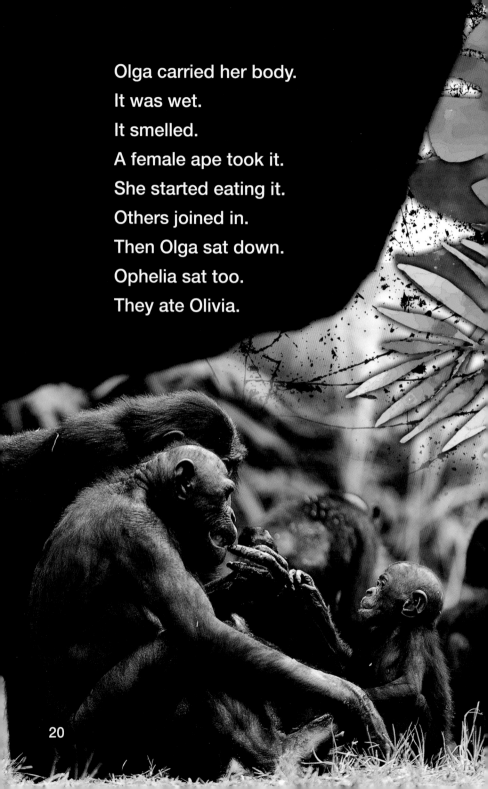

Olga carried her body.

It was wet.

It smelled.

A female ape took it.

She started eating it.

Others joined in.

Then Olga sat down.

Ophelia sat too.

They ate Olivia.

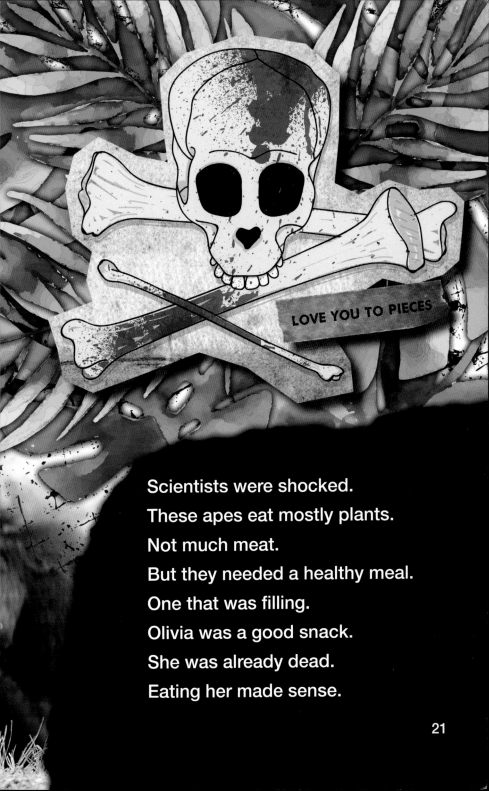

LOVE YOU TO PIECES

Scientists were shocked.

These apes eat mostly plants.

Not much meat.

But they needed a healthy meal.

One that was filling.

Olivia was a good snack.

She was already dead.

Eating her made sense.

21

Tiger *salamanders*.

They are *amphibians*.

Some eat each other.

There are two types.

Normal and cannibal.

Cannibals have big heads.

Wide mouths.

Long jaws.

Sharp teeth.

They eat the normal ones.

Why?

For *protein*.

It builds strong bones.

And keeps the body working.

XTREME KILLERS

Golden Poison Dart Frog
These tiny frogs have
enough poison to kill
ten people.

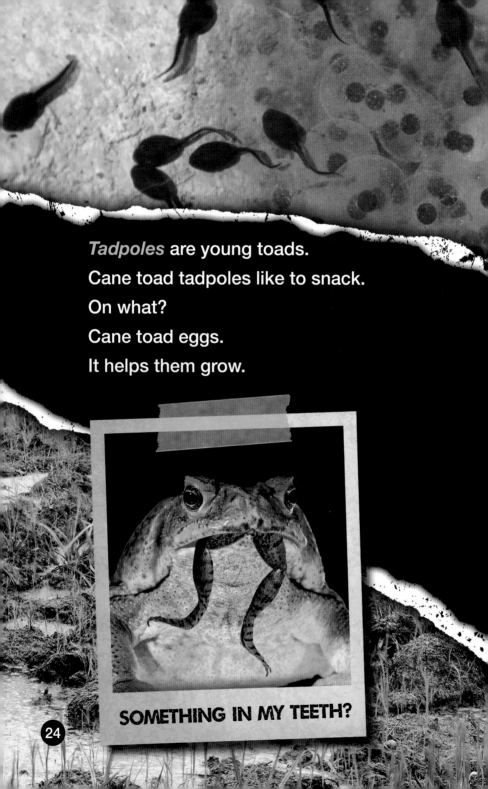

Tadpoles are young toads.

Cane toad tadpoles like to snack.

On what?

Cane toad eggs.

It helps them grow.

SOMETHING IN MY TEETH?

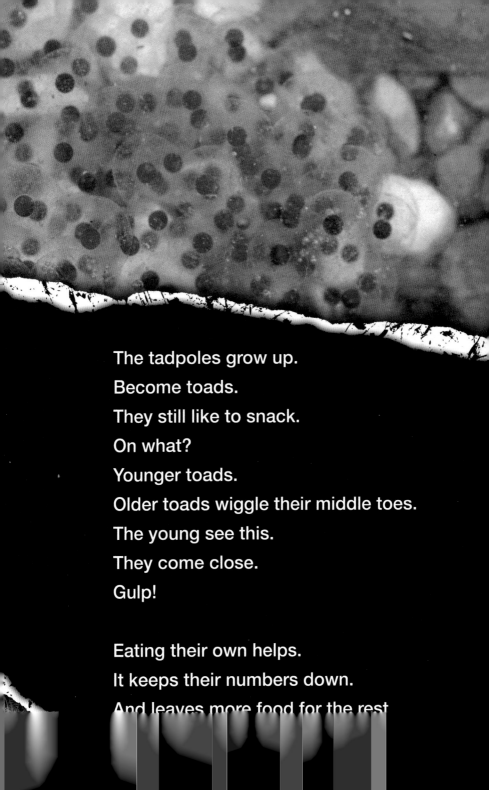

The tadpoles grow up.

Become toads.

They still like to snack.

On what?

Younger toads.

Older toads wiggle their middle toes.

The young see this.

They come close.

Gulp!

Eating their own helps.

It keeps their numbers down.

And leaves more food for the rest.

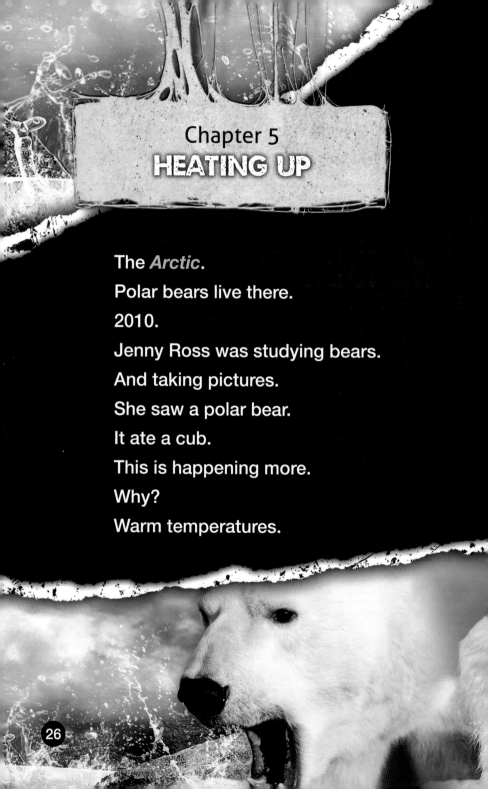

Chapter 5
HEATING UP

The *Arctic*.

Polar bears live there.

2010.

Jenny Ross was studying bears.

And taking pictures.

She saw a polar bear.

It ate a cub.

This is happening more.

Why?

Warm temperatures.

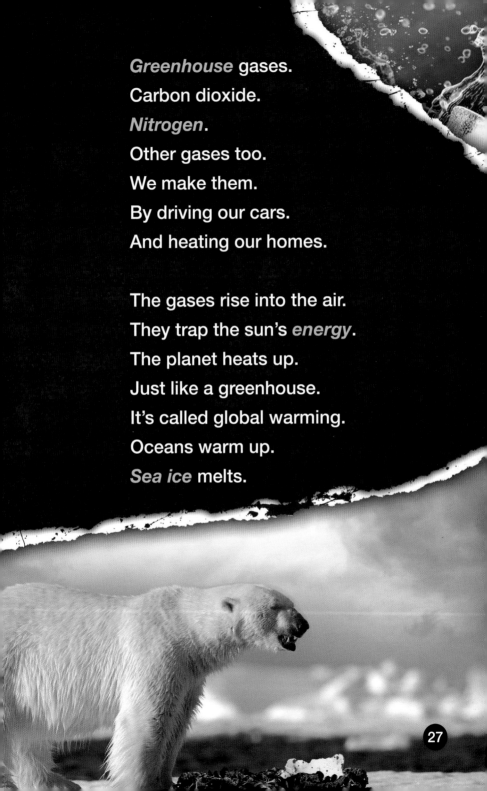

Greenhouse gases.

Carbon dioxide.

Nitrogen.

Other gases too.

We make them.

By driving our cars.

And heating our homes.

The gases rise into the air.

They trap the sun's *energy*.

The planet heats up.

Just like a greenhouse.

It's called global warming.

Oceans warm up.

Sea ice melts.

Polar bears need sea ice.

They eat seals.

But there's less ice.

It is hard to get out to the seals.

Polar bears get stuck on land.

So they eat cubs instead.

It seems mean.

But the bears are dying out.

Trying to survive.

The heat affects lobsters too.

The Atlantic Ocean is warmer.

Lobsters have moved north.

There are more in one place.

Females lay more eggs.

Many don't grow up.

They get eaten.

By hungry lobsters.

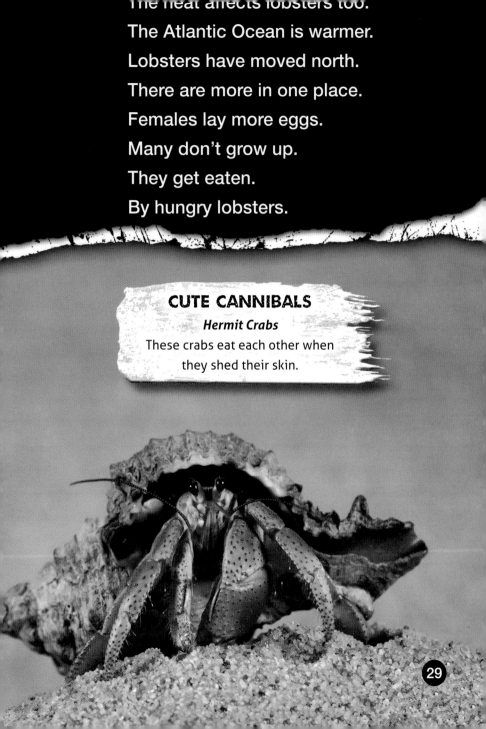

CUTE CANNIBALS

Hermit Crabs

These crabs eat each other when they shed their skin.

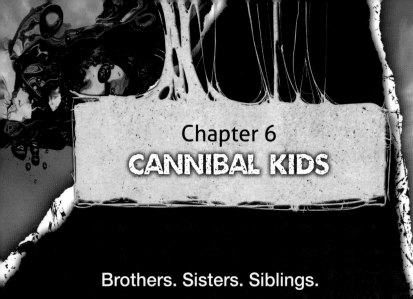

Chapter 6
CANNIBAL KIDS

Brothers. Sisters. Siblings.
They play. And fight.

Animal siblings do the same thing.
But it can turn ugly.
They may eat each other.
Some start early.

Sand tiger sharks do.
They eat each other before
they are born.
The babies are inside the mother.
The oldest *embryo* is the strongest.
The first to grow teeth.
It eats the others.

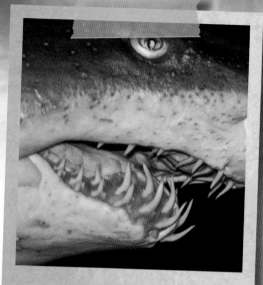

PEARLY WHITES

Wasps eat each other too.

Brothers and sisters do it a lot.

They fight each other.

One dies.

It falls to the ground.

The other lands.

And eats the body.

Ladybugs.

They are pretty.

Colorful.

But they are deadly too.

Young ladybugs stay close.

Sit near their siblings' eggs.

Then they eat them.

Chapter 7
POWER PLAY

Botswana.

A country in Africa.

Lions fight in the bush.

There are five of them.

Four males.

One female.

They trap her.

She's from another *pride*.

Or family.

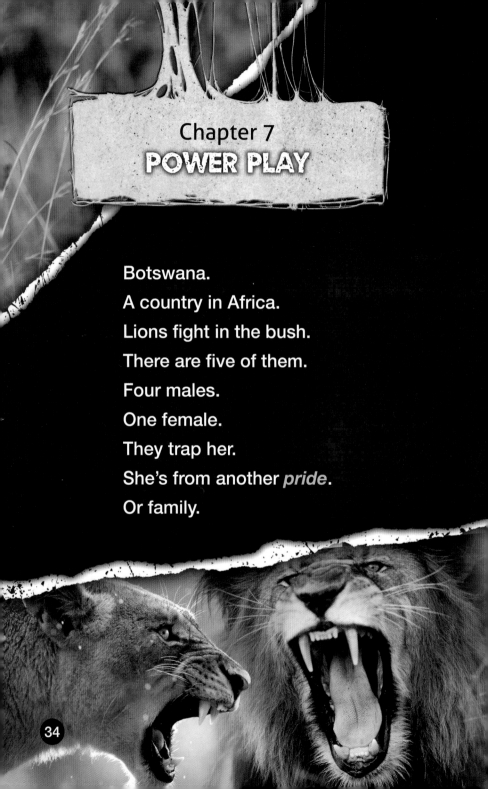

It is their land.

The female was hunting on it.

So they attack.

They rip into her.

Claws.

Teeth.

They eat her.

While she is still alive.

Lions will eat their own.

To defend their home.

And their hunting grounds.

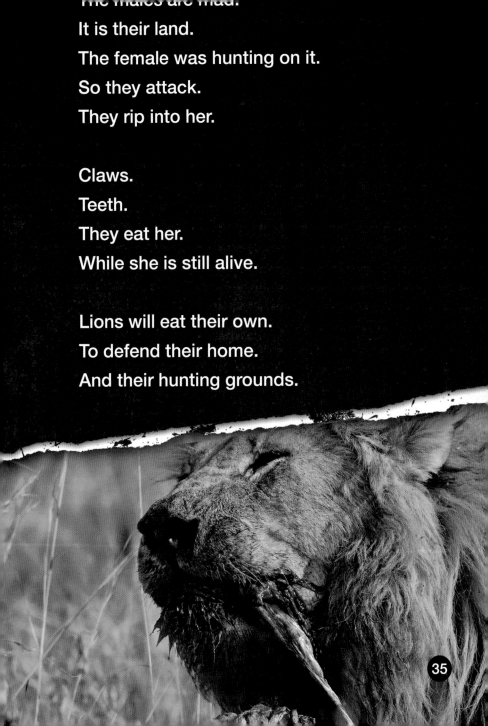

Cannibalism shows power.

A young male lion.

He wants to be king.

To lead.

But first he has to fight.

He must *defeat* the older king.

The younger lion wins.

He takes over.

The new king acts fast.

Kills the other's cubs.

Eats them.

Makes room for his own cubs.

I DON'T PLAY NICE

Hamsters are cute.

Cruel too.

Like the lion.

They fight for their space.

Don't put two in the same cage.

Only one will live.

Chapter 8
DEADLY LOVE

The redback spider.

A kind of black widow.

With a red spot on its belly.

Its bite is deadly.

For male redbacks.

The spiders mate.

The female kills the male.

Then she eats him.

Other spiders kill their mates.

So do scorpions.

Some insects do it.

Amphipods too.

DON'T CALL ME SHRIMP

We can only guess.

Females get hungry.

The hungrier they get.

The meaner they get.

Males are a healthy meal.

Their meat makes the females stronger.

That helps them lay eggs.

Some males know they will die.

Like the orb spider.

The female bites him.

He lets her.

The longer she chews the better.

It gives the male time to mate.

More time equals more eggs.

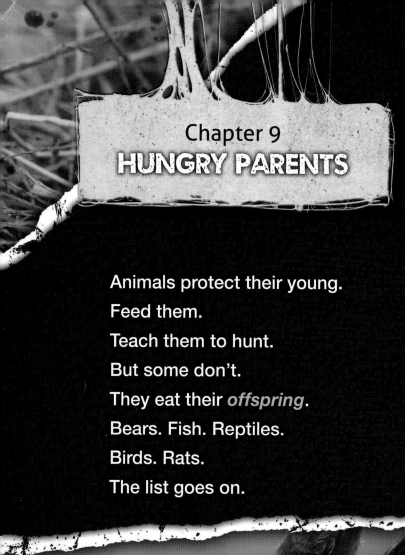

Chapter 9
HUNGRY PARENTS

Animals protect their young.

Feed them.

Teach them to hunt.

But some don't.

They eat their *offspring*.

Bears. Fish. Reptiles.

Birds. Rats.

The list goes on.

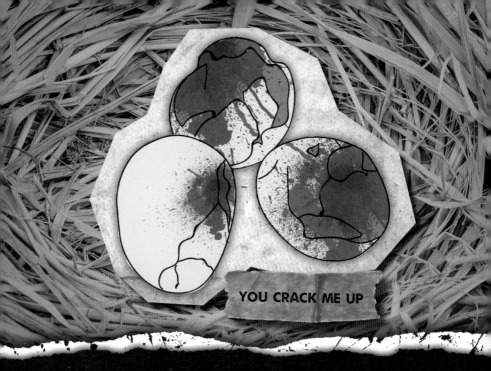

YOU CRACK ME UP

Eating offspring is common.

The weak may die.

Some take too long to grow up.

Time a parent doesn't have.

It uses up too much energy.

So they eat their young.

The meal is healthy.

It gives parents time.

And energy.

They can hunt.

Protect their home.

And raise stronger babies.

CUTE CANNIBALS

Hedgehogs

A mother will eat her young if danger is near.
She eats them so another animal won't.

Many *mammal* moms are baby killers.

It sounds cruel.

But it's true.

Moms can't nurse if they are weak.

Young animals are a good snack.

Moms can produce more milk.

And give it to their other offspring.

Hens eat their eggs.

The eggs are packed with vitamins.

It helps the hens.

They lay stronger eggs.

The shells won't crack.

That helps the new chicks survive.

Dads also kill young.

Papa grizzly bears.

They will eat their cubs.

Why?

The cubs make a mistake.

Try to eat their dad's food.

Bass.

A fish.

The male protects the young.

But he eats some when they grow up.

It helps him live.

And leaves stronger fish.

Only the fastest swim away.

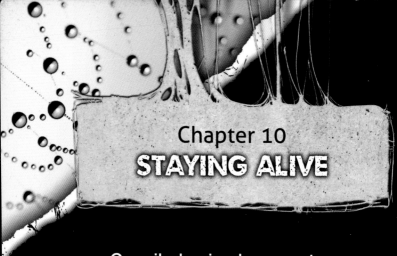

Cannibal animals are not mean.

They eat each other.

But there are reasons.

To reduce numbers.

Stay healthy.

It's all about surviving.

Living another day.

Or year.

Eating their own kind helps.

The strong can grow stronger.

Have more food to eat.

Find the best mate.

It makes sense in the wild.

Only the toughest survive.

XTREME KILLERS

Soul-Sucking Dementor
This wasp stings.
It turns cockroaches
into zombies.

49

GLOSSARY

amphibian: an animal that lives on land and in water, like a frog

amphipod: small sea or freshwater animals with a hard shell and tall, narrow bodies

Arctic: northernmost region of Earth

cannibal: an animal that eats its own kind

carbon dioxide: a gas present in the air that is absorbed by plants

copepod: tiny sea or freshwater animals with a hard shell and six legs

defeat: to beat or win

embryo: unborn baby in the first days or weeks of growth

energy: force, power

global warming: increase in Earth's temperature caused by trapped gases

greenhouse: a room where heat can be trapped to grow plants

mammal: an animal that feeds milk to its babies and usually has hair or fur

nitrogen: air is 78 percent of this gas

offspring: an animal's young

pride: a group of lions

protein: essential substance found in some foods

salamander: a small amphibian with smooth skin

sea ice: frozen seawater that floats on the surface

tadpole: young amphibian after hatching from an egg

tagged: put an ID tag on an animal

TUSKEGEE AIRMEN

Chapter 1
RED TAILS

1944.
World War II.
Up in the sky.
U.S. planes.
All are *bombers*.
They have a job.
To blow up an oil field.
It will hurt the enemy.
Slow down the war.

The planes are big.
And loud.
They are slow.
Easy targets.

One man would not give up.
Yancey Williams.
He was black.
And a pilot.
He had a goal.
To join the U.S. Army Air Corps.
He passed the tests.
The Army still said no.
He went to court.
Fought for his *rights*.
It worked.

The Army changed its rules.
It did not want a court fight.
So it made a new unit.
The 99th Pursuit *Squadron*.
A group of planes.
Flown by blacks.
Williams saw this as a win.
He joined the unit.

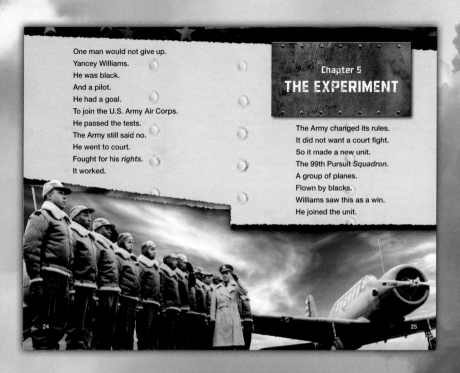

March 7, 1942.
A big day at Tuskegee.
The first class earned its wings.
Five men.
All ready to fly.

Who would lead them?
Benjamin O. Davis Jr.
He went to the U.S. Military Academy.
All the other *cadets* were white.
They did not talk to him.
But he stayed.
Studied hard.
And *graduated*.

Davis became an officer.
The Army chose him.
He would lead the 99th.
He had one goal.
"To lead this squadron to victory."

red rhino
books®
NONFICTION

9781680210293

9781680210286

9781680210309

9781680210330

9781680210361

9781680210323

9781680210316

9781680210538

9781680210347

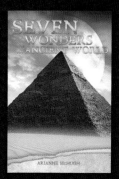

9781680210354

9781680210491

9781680210521

9781680210378

9781680210484

MORE
TITLES
COMING
SOON